Couples: From Gary to Montreal (via the World)

Couples: From Gary to Montreal (via the World)

Stefan Toma

Library of Congress Control Number:		2021912285
ISBN:	Hardcover	978-1-6641-8062-8
	Softcover	978-1-6641-8061-1
	eBook	978-1-6641-8060-4

Print information available on the last page.

Rev. date: 06/21/2021

To order additional copies of this book, contact:
Xlibris
844-714-8691
www.Xlibris.com
Orders@Xlibris.com
826589

CONTENTS

CHAPTER 1

Mom and Dad (The Original COUPLE from Gary)

JUST A QUICK look at my background, both of my parents, as well as my brother and I were born in the same city as Michael Jackson and Richard Hatcher—plus many other Tomas and Hollopeters—Gary, Indiana. The Hollopeters had been in the neighborhood, probably since shortly after the *Mayflower* and the Tomas arrived early in the century from Romania. My trip starts in June of 1953 when my family moved to Arizona. My brother had spent most of the winters until then in the hospital with bronchitis, and the doctor had told my folks that if they wanted to see him grow up and be healthy, they should change climate. So that winter we visited Miami and, I don't know why, but that summer we moved, for good, not to Miami but to Phoenix, Arizona, and sixty-five years later I believe I can say the doctor was right because my brother was not sick another day of his life. He was in the hospital again, but for different reasons, such as driving off the side of a mountain!

My life, especially my early life (first twenty-five years), always included my parents, and just before my father's ninety-fifth birthday, I was thinking about him one day, laughing at certain things that I didn't laugh at when they happened, and I decided to check with him to see if he remembered them. So I wrote to him:

Dear Dad,

I was remembering some things that happened between us or that we did together and I decided to share them with you. Maybe you'll remember some of them; maybe all of them.

The oldest memory I have was being lifted up to see our new baby, my brother. Then the next thing was when a puppy came to our door and you said that if he stayed for a couple of days that we could keep him, which he did and which we did. And then came the question of what we would call him, and you said, "That's easy. We'll call him what he is—a moocher." And so it was: Moocher!

I also remember leaving Gary! Aunt Inee, my mom's oldest sister, and Uncle Paul went to the Chicago airport to see us off, and a few hours later we were in a small motel in the desert city of Tempe, in Arizona. Our way of living really changed, and I often wonder what life would have been like if we stayed in Gary. However, Phoenix, where we finally settled, was definitely good for us.

That first winter, it really seemed warm to us, and I remember the day after you bought me some new suede shoes for school. We all left the house together and there was frost on the ground. It looked so nice. I started to run around on it, and you really got mad because I was going to ruin my new suede shoes and you chased me until you cornered me in the storage room.

Do you remember the time we went to the Teepee Restaurant together and I ordered a chile relleno and a Coke, and you said, "Come on! You can't have Coke with Mexican food. You have to have a beer." So it was: I had beer, but it was one of the last— I preferred wine!

Then there was the time that I was playing a record rather early in the morning that went *pa pa pa pa pa pa pa pa pa pa pa pa pa pa pa pa pa pa pa pa*, and you walked into the family room, and we heard a long scratch, which left the record unplayable. I have no idea what you had against *pa pa pas*, but in a similar vein, we had a glass wind chime in the carport, and one afternoon it got a quite windy and just after we sat down for dinner, you got up, went out to the carport, we heard a crash and you came back and began to enjoy your dinner.

Then I remember one day you were telling me, "I don't want you to ever make fun of your brother again. You chose to go to university and he chose to go to work." And even though I didn't remember ever making fun of him, I'm sure I never did again.

Then there were the times we drove through the San Francisco mountains and you said, "Enjoy it. This will probably be the last time we'll be here together!" It wasn't the last time, and I think you said it about five times, on different occasions.

For my fortieth birthday, we went to Bogota and you scared the hell out of me when the altitude got to you! You ran upstairs at Augusto's cousin's house completely out of breath. However, ten minutes later you were back downstairs dancing, and very well, I must say— I'd never seen you on the dance floor before!

What I most remember from my trips to Romania was that the first day that we were there together, you didn't understand a word, then the next day you began to understand a lot more, and two days later you understood everything. You conversed and answered all questions that we were asked without a pause, and it was still too difficult for me.

Then, when we were traveling around the country, in Agris Mic (Little Agrish), Romania, we ran into a man who I asked where the cemetery was, and he answered very gruffly, "Why do you want to go to the cemetery?" When we replied that we wanted to see the names of relatives that might be there, because our grandfather was from Agris, he then asked the name of our grandfather. We answered, "Daniel Toma," and he answered, again very gruffly, "he's never been here." And then he warmed up and said, "Go to Agris Mare (Big Agrish), and there you will find your relatives' graves." We were puzzled by his answer but soon we finally understood that Agris Mic (little Agrish) was a Hungarian village and Agris Mare was Romanian (or vice-versa).

When I first started working with jewelry and you came to see me, in Rome, I asked Mom to see her wedding ring and I said to her, "Oh, it's beautiful! I didn't know they made diamonds that small."

And, do you remember:

- In Mexico City, walking down Insurjentes to the *Zocalo* with Mom when suddenly I turned bright red and you said, "Stef, what's wrong?" but I could barely talk. It was the first and last time I was pinched in public (by a very beautiful girl, I might add).
- Driving from Geneva to Zurich with Mom and I? I was going around 80 mph (over 100 kilometers per hour) and still everybody was passing me.
- You and Mom arriving in Italy and eating at the trattoria Carbonara in Roma and at various restaurants in the Castelli Romani Region.
- When we climbed South Mountain and our puppy (named by you, Itchy) stepped on a cactus and you had to carry him all the way up and then down the mountain, and on the same walk

I tripped on a stone and when I picked it up, there was a huge tarantula on it.

- When we went to get Roscoe, our Dalmatian, we felt we were being watched and then we saw that there were turkeys on the second floor, all of them looking down on us,
- When you met Rose for the first time and asked her what she would like to do for her first time in Phoenix, so seven of us drove to Las Vegas and then we left together for Montreal to be married.
- Your sixtieth wedding anniversary and our leaving the big shindig, also in Las Vegas. We left at around midnight and arrived at JFK at seven in the morning of September 11, 2001.
- When you visited me in San Juan and my friends, the Rosens, took you for the weekend to the Virgin Islands and that evening you learned to play Progressive Gin? That was about fifty years ago, and we're still playing it.

I'll send you another page someday. Meanwhile, have a very merry Christmas with Ray and Anita, Danny and Dana, Nicolae, Mimmo, Patrick, Emily, and Beauregard (their dog).

My brother had moved to Oregon where he lived for about twenty years before settling in Oxford, Mississippi, where his older son had made his home. The following is one of the last things I sent him.

Happy Birthday . . . DAD

It's great you've seen March fourth with a grin
And I'm glad you're feeling well
We wish you many fourths again,
'Cause you have so much to tell.

We see you getting younger
And more and more alive,
So enjoy all those around you,
But please, Dad, do not drive.

We know you're in good company,
And we hope your sky's not gray,
Of course it really can't be,
with the kids, Anita and Ray.

From Montreal and Arzier,
We send you hugs and love,
We know you're well protected,
and favored by him above.

La multi ani (May you live many years) and celebrations,
You deserve to dance and jive,
And show everyone you know,
You're a jewel and ninety-five

My father died when I was in Egypt. I never realized how much I would miss him and my mom until they were both gone!

My mother died when I was in Saudi. I knew that she was in the hospital, so when the phone rang at 2:00 in the morning, I said something under my breath and answered the phone to find out she had just passed away. I wrote this for her on my flights to Oregon, where she and my father had lived, near my brother, the last couple of years.

In the name of the Father, the Son, and the Holy Spirit, Lord, hear me:

TO OUR MOTHER, OR OTHER

With loved ones who you gave to us
Be they neighbor, friend, or clan,
Give us love to share with all
And help them when we can.

And when those who are close to us
Yet find their world in strife
Help us help them understand
You've prepared for them a better life.

STEFAN TOMA

O daughter, aunt, O father,
O friend, O foe, O son,
O mother, sister, brother
In spirit and faith we're one.

I've felt your warmth beside me
Since birth or yesterday
But now God wants to take you
As he promised us in his way

So let us mourn together
For those we love who leave
But let us mourn in faith and hope
And not give in and grieve

For if we've learned about you, Lord
We know our future is bright
And though you've taken a loved one
We know that all is right

From touchable to spirit
Man, woman, girl, and boy
At the right time leaves and goes to you
And their pain melts into joy

So now we're here together
And I hold you all so dear
So together let's say, Bye, Mom,
without any reason to fear.

And it's really all right for all of us
To say it with a tear.
Amin

I want to mention that my mom once asked me why I didn't invite her to go to Romania with my dad and me. I was surprised by the question and my answer was, "Because I was sure you wouldn't want to go with us," to which she answered, "You're absolutely right, but you could have at least invited me!" And she's absolutely right, I could/SHOULD have invited her.

And she surprised us when, after seeing an article in the newspaper, she went with a neighbor lady to the Mormon temple in Mesa, Arizona, and dug up a big orange tree, which she planted in our back yard and which gave us oranges every year for years! This was just to let you know where I got the idea of answering newspaper articles.

CHAPTER 2

My First of a Couple of Trips (By Myself (Sort Of)

WHEN I WAS thirteen years old, I took my first trip by myself. I had worked as a slop boy—that's what they called those of us who worked cleaning the kitchen in the grade school I was attending. I also had a paper route, and I saved up a little over 100 dollars (well, it seemed to me a fortune). Anyway, I decided I wanted to go visit a friend of mine, my grandparents, and my cousins. My dad agreed, but my mother didn't think it was such "a hot idea." Anyway my father bought me a round-trip ticket on the bus to Fayetteville, Arkansas, the Florida Everglades, and Chicago, which is just a few miles from Gary, and back to Phoenix. In all, I was on the bus for over a week, and I was gone for about two and a half months, and the bus ticket cost us just $99. I had a safe and good trip, and it prepared me for a life of travels and work. I continued to work as a slop boy. I picked cotton and strawberries and even walked, as if I were naked, in a barrel to advertise, I don't remember exactly what.

So as soon as classes ended, I took off! My first stop was in Fayetteville, Arkansas, to visit Bill, my best friend from school. His mother had just remarried, and he and his sisters moved to Arkansas with his mother and new father. The things I most remember were the first day we worked all day in the farms, digging and picking. That evening at the dinner table, I felt something on the back of my neck and I said to them, "Do I have something here?"

His mom got up and came over to look. She played around with my neck and said, "Don't move." Then she showed me something, saying, "It's nothing—just a tick."

"A tick!" I said. "I thought only dogs got ticks." Well, now you know, and there are probably more, so before you go to bed, check and see and if you have more. Take them out and make sure you get the whole body out because they can really make you sick, especially if you leave the head! So that night before I went to bed, I found about six more—three of which I had to take out myself because they were in a very private part of the body, including some very private places.

The next day we were excused from working on the farm, and Bill asked me if I wanted to go into a cave he'd found. Of course I wanted to go! It sounded like the most interesting thing we could do. "It wasn't far," he explained, "but it's rather difficult to get into." Why? You'll see. A few minutes later, he said, "We arrived."

"Where?" I said.

"Right here," he said as he pulled back some plants, which hid a rather small hole.

"That's it?"

"Well, this is the hard part. It gets bigger and better as you go through it."

And he was right. After a few very small caverns, the rooms became much larger, BUT we had to go through the small ones to get in and out, and, I must say, it was very difficult. I felt I knew what it was like to be about to die. But it was worth it. It was one of the first things I can say I'll never forget.

So our day was almost ended. "Let's go visit a friend," he said.

"Who?" I said.

"You'll see," he said, and what a friend he had! She was beautiful! I had never imagined someone our age could have such a beautiful girl friend. I felt like I was in a movie the rest of the day!

Then I left for my grandparents in Florida, the Everglades—at least it looked like the Everglades. I wasn't too much for fishing, but we fished every day, and the three things I most remember from my stay were, of course, my grandmother's cooking was number one. Two was, once when we were fishing, something very strong began to pull on my line. My grandfather grabbed the rod and said, "You've got a biggie!" and then all of a sudden a row of teeth about a meter long appeared. "Wow, it's a garfish!" my grandfather shouted, "and a big one at that!" It was definitely the scariest thing I'd ever seen, to date that is. It had a row of teeth that I remember, exaggeratedly, being about two or three feet long. And the third thing I remember was my grandmother looking at the calendar. She turned the page and upon turning it, she yelled, "What is this!" And it was the biggest SCORPION I'VE EVER SEEN and I've seen a lot of them.

And from there, I went to Gary, Indiana, via Chicago. And after spending a month with my cousins, I returned to Phoenix, where I repeated all the above stories until people started saying, "Yeah, yeah, we've heard about it a hundred times already."

CHAPTER 3

My Brother and My Sister-in-Law (A Really Nice and a Really Young Couple)

MY BROTHER, RAY, got married on Valentine's Day. She was seventeen and he had just turned eighteen. They finished high school and my poor brother went to work the day, really, the day he graduated. That was one of the things they had to agree upon before they set the date for the wedding, that they both would finish high school before they would look for work.

Here is a poem I sent them for their fiftieth wedding anniversary. Believe me, they've been through a lot, but they've had a good life as have their kids, and their kids' kids! (And very soon, their kids' kids' kids.)

Anita and Ray (Don't Worry, There Aren't Many More Poems!)

Anita, young and perfect
From El Paso came to town
Young, pretty, and promising
A handsome young boy she found

Raymond was his name, it was,
And from Rayray it stayed at Ray,
Though young, he knew a good thing
And together they chose their way

The family met her with delight
When they saw her style and face
She quickly evolved to be with us
And offered wisdom and grace!

They soon became three from two
And from there the number grew
A new lad made number four
With bonds so strong, forever more

The two then learned in their way
They worked hard to make their nest
Slowly but surely they had
A family at par with the best

From the heat one day they parted
To beauty and peace in the north
Enabled by work and success
A new life for all then came forth

They built and they grew in faith
The old and the new to embrace
Listening to their blood and beyond
Higher visions changed their face

From youth together they traveled
Roads sunny, dangerous, and misty
Avoiding mines and barricades
Today they're both well and safe at sixty

So if in the past you doubted
Either of these wonderful souls
Take a deep breath and then look
Both youngsters have met all their goals

To RAY and ANITA, with all our love from your brother and family.

CHAPTER 4

My Second of a Couple of Trips (To Colombia with Augusto)

THERE WAS A very pretty young lady in my Spanish class. One day, after the first week of classes, I asked her if she had time to have a Coke with me. She said she would and I was the happiest kid on campus. So we went to the cafeteria and while we were there, I asked her out. However, she turned me down because she had a boyfriend (I was no longer the happiest boy on campus). To make the long story short (2MLSS), I eventually met the boyfriend, Augusto, and we became friends, and the three of us decided to spend the summer in Bogota at his home.

Come summer and she couldn't go, but I decided to go anyway, and getting there was half the fun. My family drove us to Mexico, where we had lunch, and then Augusto and I took a taxi to the airport in Mexico. About halfway there, we ran out of gas in the middle of nowhere, and the taxi man, after swearing a little, jumped up and out of the car and ran down the dusty road. When we lost sight of him, we decided very quickly that the only thing we could do was to tag down another taxi, if one came by, because we seemed to be the only ones going to the airport. Ten or fifteen minutes later, a car finally came by. It stopped and out jumped the taxi driver carrying a small bottle of gasoline, which he assured us was enough to get us to the airport. It was and we caught our flight to Ciudad de Mexico, of course, after stopping in Mazatlan, Culiacan, Ciudad Obregon, and Guadalajara. Of course, we also had yet to stop in Guatemala, San Salvador, Managua, and Panama before arriving in Bogota.

From Mexico we flew to Guatemala City, where we spent the night with a wonderful family. I remember the daughter made quite an impression on me, and when I told Augusto that I thought she was really pretty, his comment was, "Yes, but she's just a common beauty!" That night before we went to bed, we both had a couple of drinks. I had originally said, "No, thank you," and was immediately told by Augusto that I could not say no because they were offering me a very fine whiskey and that I would be insulting them if I turned it down (even though I had never in my life had a drop of alcohol). The next morning we left the house early so that we could see Antigua, the original capital and a lovely city. Before we reached Antigua, we stopped at a small roadside restaurant for a quick breakfast. I wasn't feeling too well because of the drinks I had the night before. Our "driver," or should I say our host, asked the waiter what was on the breakfast menu, and the second I heard him say "Morcilla," blood sausage, I puked all over my shoes! And I don't usually use this word, but I did not throw up, I puked.

We visited not only Antigua, but Guatemala City and the lake region, which was gorgeous, and we made it to the airport just in time. When we reached Managua, I was still sick. On one hand, going through customs seemed grueling, but we had such a welcoming that I forgot about feeling bad, at least until we got through customs.

A couple of weeks earlier, my father had been approached by the chamber of commerce to see if he would like to entertain a group of Nicaraguans on the weekend. He said yes and we had about thirteen of them to dinner. They were all around our age, and we all had a good time, and when they heard that we would be traveling to Bogota, they invited us to stop in Nicaragua on the way.

We had a wonderful time in Managua, but the bus trip after we arrived at the airport was a killer. I was still quite sick to my stomach. But I recovered and our trip to the beach the next day was unforgettable. One of the fellows' parents had a house on the beach. We all went and as soon as I jumped into the sea, I had to ask if they had a bathroom in the house. He said yes, there were two of them and one of them was in the back of the house and was easy to find because it was the only door in the back of the house. So I ran like hell toward the house and pulling down my swimming suit, I reached the door, which I grabbed to open and couldn't wait to sit down. But just as I was about to hit the seat, for some reason I decided I better check it out for bugs. It had just dawned on me that the house had not been used for the last four months, and just as I reached down to check out the back of the toilet seat, a huge dragon stuck out his head and started coming out of the toilet. I yelled (or screamed bloody murder, which I learned only after this happened) and slammed the door shut and went running back to the shore where everyone laughed, and they ran back to the house with me and they even laughed more when they saw a huge iguana jump back into the toilet.

A few days later we overnighted in Panama City, which then was the poorest capital city I had seen for many years. (I was there several years later to find it quite nice.) The next morning we arrived in Bogota, and my life changed completely. I was now an international person (well, a bit). I was also in an international city. Augusto lived in the middle of a big town with his mother, father, and sister. Every day we went to visit an uncle or a cousin, and too soon the summer was over (although I don't remember it being warm even one day—Bogota is at 3,000 feet above sea level), and too soon we were on our way back to Phoenix.

Augusto became a prominent part of my life, a real brother who took good care of my parents for many years. He eventually married Debbie, and we remained good friends. They had two boys, Phillip and Christopher, and I was drawn toward them even more than normal because when they talked, they used the same intonations and had the same vocabulary as our mother.

CHAPTER 5

*El Senor Me Escucho, Our Father Listened to Me (The First of a Couple, Two or Three Times)

I T WAS AUTUMN, the university had started and I was depressed. My classes were giving me a hard time and I couldn't shake it. Anyway, one Sunday after church, I decided to pray about it, which was something new—not saying prayers, but to ask for help for something specific. Basically, I remember saying, "Please, God, get me out of here. I need some time for only me, not the university."

Two or three days later when I arrived home, I found a letter in the mailbox from the Peace Corps. Surely it was my rejection letter! More or less it said, "Dear Mr. Toma, training will start in October, and when it's over you will be sent to Colombia!" I thought, it's not possible, but just in case, the next day I did something, which immediately took me out of my depression. First, I called them (at the Peace Corps) just in case I hadn't read the letter right, and then I dropped all of my classes. I was ecstatic and a short time later I was in the Caribbean, thrilled with my new direction. At the end of the first week, I had a medical checkup and I was told that I had an ulcer that was probably from my depression and it might not be good for me to continue, so they "regretted to tell me but that they would give me a ticket back to Phoenix and that I should leave as soon as possible." Do you know what it means to be depressed? You know? Well, I was not in the least bit depressed!

CHAPTER 6

A Couple of a Couple of Kids

I TOOK SPANISH again the next year and enjoyed it even more, and when my junior year ended, I had saved up enough money to go to Mexico for summer school if I could find someplace to stay that wasn't expensive. One night I met some people from Mexico City and one of the girls I met told me I could probably stay with her mother for the first couple of weeks while I looked for an inexpensive place to stay. I enjoyed my stay with la senora, but I was told I would have to leave as soon as her daughter came home because she was engaged and it would not be correct for me to stay. As luck would have it, when Mayu (the daughter) arrived the same day, I moved in with her fiancé, Ricardo, and we all became friends for life.

They got married about three weeks later and left the same day for Tijuana. I was still going to the university and I left for San Diego the following morning, hitchhiking! It was one of two times I hitchhiked in my life, and I was only worried once and that was when I was let out near a small city in the middle of the desert at dusk, but luckily I was picked up almost immediately by a car going to downtown San Diego.

I arrived and decided to cross the border right away. We had a very happy reunion, and the next morning we visited Tijuana together and after a couple of hours they asked me if I was hungry. I said yes and they asked me what I wanted to eat. Something special? I said no, anything, and they said, "Okay, why don't we go to the same place we had gone to the night before?"

I said, "I don't understand what you're saying. I arrived after dinner last night." They laughed and said, "All right, we'll choose." We walked a bit and then we were in front of a restaurant and they said, "Let's go in here." After we went in they said, "How does it look?" I said fine, even familiar, and they laughed. "Does it really look familiar?" they said.

"Now that you mention it, yes, but last night was the first time I was in Tijuana. And last night after you had several drinks, we had dinner here." That's why it looks familiar! Needless to say, I was a bit SHOCKED! Anyway, it was Sunday so I left for Phoenix in the afternoon so I could go to my Monday classes, as I had promised my parents. They stayed in Tijuana and eventually both found jobs in San Diego. They also had two children, Esteban and Rodrigo, who are still friends with my nephews, Danny and Rory (and me).

Some years later they came to NYC where they stayed with me until they found a place big enough for the four of them. And as I write this, I just received a note from their youngest son, who now lives in Chicago.

CHAPTER 7

Peace Corps (A Couple of Days that Changed My Life)

<hr/>

I F YOU HAVE read chapter 5 you've already read about my entire Peace Corps career.

CHAPTER 8

My First Career (of a Couple, Two or Three)

WHEN I RETURNED to Phoenix from the Peace Corps, I started looking for a job right away. At one point I saw an article in the *Phoenix Gazette* saying that Aeronaves de Mexico was opening a route between Ciudad de Mexico and Phoenix beginning in May. I read the article a couple of times and said to myself, "What the hell, that's what I would like to do." So I wrote a letter to them, requesting an interview. I didn't hear from them so when I saw another article that gave the schedules and announcing the date of their first flights, I gave up. One day I was mowing the lawn when my mother came and told me I had a call from the airlines. I don't think I had told her that I had I applied to work for them, so I imagine I told her when she asked me why they were calling I just said, "It's to tell me to go jump in the lake."

"Hello, Senor Toma, I'm calling from Aeronaves de Mexico, can you come to the airport to talk to us?"

"Of course, I would be happy to go."

"Could you come tomorrow, at about one o'clock?"

"Of course!"

"Come to the old terminal."

My mother then asked me what they said. "You'll never believe it. I'm going for an interview, TOMORROW!" My excitement ended there! It was the first time I'd ever been to a real interview! My appointment was at 13:00, and I arrived at around 12:45. Please, God, have them speak to me in English!

At 12:55, "Mr. Toma?"

"Yes?"

"Pase Ud. (Come in.)"

I don't remember the interview, but it was all in Spanish. Oh well, I tried. But I didn't give up until Sunday! My dad said, "Don't worry, your next interview will be better."

"I hope so."

RING! "Hello, just a moment . . . It's for you," my dad said.

"Who?"

"I don't know and he didn't say."

"Allo, Sr. Toma, siento mucho llamarle el Domingo, pero podria Ud. empezar manana?"

"Si, si, at what time?"

"A las 8:00. Va bien?"

"Si!"

"I'll see you then. Hasta mañana."

"Hasta Mañana."*

[Hello, Mr. Toma, I'm very sorry to call you on a Sunday, but would you be able to start work tomorrow?" "Yes, yes, at what time?" "At 8:00, would that be all right?" "See you tomorrow." "See you tomorrow."]

You have no idea, actually, I had no idea how this affected my approach to speaking to people in future interviews. I loved my new job, however, I looked at the university the way most people look at high school: It was just another necessary part of my life, so even though I loved working for Aeronaves, I knew I would have to figure out what I'd do when school started in the fall. I repeat, I felt happy every day while I worked there! Oh well. "AERONAVES DE MEXICO anuncia la salida se su vuelo 101 con destino a la Ciudad de Mexico, con paradas intermediadas en Mazatlan, Ciudad Obregon ETC. ETC. ETC." That was me!

CHAPTER 9

Miami, Donde Estamos? In the US! De Veras? (Where Are We? In the US! Really?)

WHEN I FINISHED my courses at ASU and Thunderbird, I decided to go to Miami. I remembered how much I had enjoyed it when I was just ten years old, and I imagined it would be even better now. Well, now that I think about it, I really wanted to go to New York, but I was sure that my folks would do everything to keep me from going because I had cousins that went there after high school and whenever they spoke about them, they whispered. So I left for Miami a few days after the last of my exams were over, with their support, more or less. I was very lucky because a few days after I arrived, I saw an advertisement in the *Miami Herald* for one of the Latin American airlines that served the area. So I wasted no time in applying and, strangely enough, they wasted no time in hiring me. Not only did I find a job, I found an apartment for a very good price, right next the airport and not that far away from the landing strip and about a fifteen-minute walk to my new office. It had a small swimming pool right under an extension of the landing strip, so every so often you either had to go underwater or go deaf.

Again I loved me new job and again no one believed me when I told them that I didn't know anyone, that I had simply answered an ad. It was a great first job (actually a second), and my colleagues were all Latin Americans, mainly Cubans and Peruvians. It wasn't a difficult job, mainly, I just answered telephone calls and made reservations.

One day the man who hired me came to where I was sitting and said that he would like to listen to how I answered the phone for a while, so I shouldn't go to lunch when I was supposed to. All of my calls went well and I was happy when the lady I reported to came by and told me, "Okay, Stefan, go to lunch." So I was very happy and I figured that he must have been happy with my calls. About 3 pm my big boss came in the office and told me, "Stefan, I'm sorry but you're fired. Don't bother to come back again!"

Of course I immediately said, "Why, what was wrong with the way I answered the phone?"

"Not a thing, but I told you I wanted to listen to you and you left."

"I left because the lady I report to told me to go to lunch."

"And I told you to answer the phone, but you decided it was more important to go to lunch, so you are fired!"

It was the only time I was ever fired. But my leaving didn't cause any problems in my office because, strangely enough, the same day he fired me, he hired his niece to take over my position. Thank God! At least he had someone who could take over my work right away.

Probably the main reason I liked Miami was the fact that everyone spoke to me in Spanish, which I loved, and I loved hearing the different accents of various countries. I especially liked to hear my colleagues, in my first job in Miami, talk among themselves. They always tried to use words that had a second meaning, a bad one, in the language of the one they were speaking with, but that was a perfectly good word in most of the Spanish-speaking countries of South and Central America. I was really impressed by the way the Cubans spoke the language. I guess I learned it pretty well though because once I was leaving Bogota and a man came up to me and showed me his ID card and said, "SECURITY, please come with me," I, of course, became very nervous because I couldn't figure out what I was being stopped for. Then he asked me what I was doing in Bogota. I told him that I was visiting friends and then he said,

"Y donde vives en la Habana? (Where do you live in Habana?)"

"What?" I said.

"En donde vives en la Habana?"

"Lo siento, pero no le entiendo. (I'm sorry, but I don't understand.)"

"EN DONDE VIVES EN LA HABANA?"

"I understand the question, but I don't understand why you are asking me, En donde vivo en la Habana. Do you understand English?" I asked him.

"Yes!"

"Yes?"

"I don't think so! Look what it says in the first page of my passport: Not good for travel to Cuba."

"Then why do you speak Spanish?"

I bit my tongue as he handed me my passport and I told him, "Because I'm smart." I don't remember what happened after that, but I made the flight back to the States.

Anyway, getting back to Miami, I started applying again and I ended up working for a couple of years for Air Canada. Besides liking my job, I had the best boss I ever had, and I tried to be like him when I had a job with a little seniority, and I'll tell you just one of the reasons I liked him: One day I asked him if I could take one of my scheduled workdays off. He said, "Yes, of course," then he said, "May I ask what for?"

"Uhhhh, yes, I want to go to an interview to become a purser."

"Oh! You think you'd like to be a flight attendant. You're already working for an airline, so you're halfway there. Anyway, go to the interview, and at the same time I'll see what I can do for you, all right?"

To make a LONG story SHORT, he checked and there was nothing available. However, I was given the right to go to either New York, Cleveland, or Vancouver for the summer (because they needed extra people during this busy season). Guess which one I chose?

Anyway, the time I spent in Miami was great. Everyone spoke Spanish—well, not everyone, but the friends I made did. I loved the Cuban restaurants and Cuban cuisine and the atmosphere, in general.

CHAPTER 10

Back to the Homeland and the End of My First Career

S INCE I WAS working for the airlines, I decided to take advantage of all the familiarization flights possible. One of the first was to Rio de Janeiro, where I immediately fell in love with the girl from Ipanema, I mean "The Girl from Ipanema." I was totally hooked on Brazilian music, and I learned Portuguese quite well in a fairly short time. (Brazilian Portuguese, that is—I still have a very difficult time understanding Portuguese Portuguese.)

I worked for Air Canada for a couple of years, and then I decided to finish my first master's degree, since I had less than one semester left. Then I went back to NYC, where I finished my first career with Ecuatoriana and Eastern Airlines. One summer I decided to take the whole summer off and go to Europe and beyond, so I started saving as much as I could until I had enough to go on a grand tour.

I thought about starting to write my memoirs about a month earlier because in reality, this would be the end of my first career with the airlines, which started miraculously in Phoenix. I only worked for four or five months with Aeronaves, but then I had experience, and experience is the most important thing you can have when you're looking for a job. No matter how much or how little you learn, it sways you in all directions and it gives you hands-on INFORMATION! I had thought of starting to write the day I left for Europe, and as usual I met my goal, but barely. So the day I was leaving should have been a very happy one. I should have felt beside myself, with happiness, anticipating my new first day, however, I didn't feel a thing! It didn't seem like I was off for anywhere, at least anywhere special. During the last two years, I had traveled so much that it usually seemed very routine, and I remember so well the day of my first trip to Bogota with Augusto, I was so excited I couldn't stand it. I spent the last night before leaving drinking Coca-Cola and dancing rancheras with my family and some friends at Nanos Lounge in South Phoenix. I finally went to bed at around two o'clock, and I was up by three taking a shower and bothering the whole family with musica Latina so loud, even the neighbors wondered what was going on.

But the day in question, I was just feeling bored out of my mind thinking of the last days in the office of financial control, which was my last airline job with Eastern Airlines. Well, come to think about it, in addition to the boredom, I was beginning to feel really quite relaxed knowing I wouldn't have to work in finance anymore. (This was my last job with the airline, and it was quite a change—

this means, I didn't enjoy it—and besides that, I always felt relaxed at the airport waiting for a flight, which hadn't been the case that day.) When I arrived at the terminal of Air Canada at JFK, I felt a very strange atmosphere, compared with my normal itineraries to Latin America. There seemed to be fewer people. There was almost no noise, and upon boarding there was nobody yelling. I didn't even hear one *mira mira* or *mira nene* (Look, look, or Look, kid), and I missed it! Well, at least the difference indicated that there was a change in the air. *Dans 20 minutes je serait dan le vol. Que nice!* (In twenty minutes I'll be on the flight. How nice!)

We had just landed in Paris, and I still didn't feel that moment of supreme happiness that I expected. Of course I felt better, but the words that best describe me until about 21:00 was "like a piece of shit!" (This was only because I was traveling without knowing where I was going! Yes, I knew the names, but I didn't know what to expect in certain places, especially the Middle East.) However, that evening I found a place to stay (for nine dollars a night—in Paris!), and I unexpectedly met up with some friends, so I suddenly became much better.

CHAPTER 11

My Last Degree (Yes, I Have a Couple of Masters)

I HAD MADE A lot of plans for this trip. In addition to Paris, I would be going to Germany, Lebanon, Greece, ROMANIA (my new old country), Portugal, Spain, back to Germany, and then home again, home again, jiggedy jig.

After my grand trip to France and Germany, I continued on to Lebanon and Greece.

In Greece I visited all of the famous landmark buildings in the center of Athens, plus I took some short cruises to enjoy some of the beaches, which I remember because on one island, they were called Paradise, Super Paradise, and Hell. In Paradise, everyone was wearing just regular men and women's bathing suits. In Super Paradise, the men wore bikinis as did most of the women, also one-piece, and in Hell, you didn't even need to wear one.

While I was in Greece, I took the train to Romania and back. It was the only time in my life that I had long hair, and it drew a lot of attention. On the train it seemed like every one that walked by me had to touch my head to see if I had a wig or if it was real, or if I was real!

I was so excited about going to Romania that as soon as I got my visa, I called my grandfather. "Grandpa! Guess where I'm going this summer."

"Where," he asked.

"Romania," I told him with a very excited voice!

"WHY, what for?" he said with a very non-excited voice.

"It's our homeland," I said.

"America is much better," he said, to which I said, "Anyway, I'll tell you all about it when I come back!"

It was the only country I visited by train. We stopped in Bulgaria on the way. As soon as we arrived, I went into a little restaurant. I sat down and the waiter came and asked if he could help me. I said yes and I asked to see the luncheon menu. "We don't have one. We only have one thing for lunch."

"Well then, I guess I'll have that." It was delicious! So I told him and asked what they would have on the evening menu.

"The same thing: we have just one dish."

So come time for the evening meal, I went to a different but very nice restaurant and voila, the same dish. Oh well, that evening I left for Bucharest.

The following morning I woke up on the train, but I was at home (for the first time). I immediately began to look for a hotel, which I found to be very inexpensive. I then found that they had given me a special visa for people of Romanian descent, which gave me the right to pay my hotel in Romanian currency at Romanian prices, which were quite low. The following day I discovered a place called the Office of Tourism for Youth (Uffizio de Turismo Pentru Tineretului). They were so nice. The fellow who I spoke to told me that he was taking a group of young men and women to the seacoast in the morning, that if I would like to go with them, I would probably have a good time. The only problem was that the train left very early in the morning. He showed me exactly where I should meet him and exactly at five minutes to six, not a minute later.

The following morning I was there at a quarter to six, and the man who was taking the group arrived at five minutes to six. He took me aboard the train and told me to sit down at a certain place and under no circumstances should I move, that he would find me. At 6:00, on the nose, you could hear the train motors go on, the doors opened, and all of Bucharest tried to find a seat! People even came through the windows that were open. And they had to stand up until we stopped and people got off, four hours later, on the coast. When we arrived at, I think it was in Craiova, if I remember, the first thing I did was to go around the village to see if I could find a place to stay. I had been told that there was no place available at the resort, but that it would be easy to find a place in the village. WRONG!

"Existe camera (Do you have a room)?"

"No!"

Existe camera?"

"No!"

"Existe camera?"

No, there wasn't a room available in the entire village, so I went back to the hotel where my new friends were staying and where we had agreed to meet so we could have lunch together. "No problem, you can stay in our room with us."

It was the only time in my life that I ever slept on a cement floor, and I mean, right on the cement, with only a sheet!

A few days later I headed back to Bucharest, the capital, to catch my train back Greece. Then I went on to Beirut, where on my second day I decided to go to AUB, the American University of Beirut. It had a great atmosphere, filled with beautiful pine trees and a beautiful view of the sea as well. Afterward I decided to go back to the part of the city I knew, but then I decided to go back to the university bookstore to see what the English/Arabic textbooks looked like. I walked for about ten minutes and all of a sudden I was face to face with a fellow that I knew, who studied with me in Arizona: Walid.

It was a very nice encounter, and the next day I met with him and he took me to the bank where Emile, another friend, was working. I did my banking, after which they gave me a tour of the center of the city. That evening things picked up again when I went to dinner with Walid and his sister, along with Emile, his sister, and his girlfriend.

I still had a week before I had to take my flight, so I checked around and found a small place announcing a bus trip to Syria, and by chance I ran across the Canadian ambassador who wanted to take a similar one. The trip was to be only four days long, leaving early in the morning and staying the first night at Crak de Chevalier, the second night in Damascus (Shams), the third night in Todmore, and last day in Petra, returning in the afternoon to Beirut, where I was still visiting my friends from graduate school.

CHAPTER 12

Roma, Toma, and My Second Career

———◇———

T HEN I FLEW from Lebanon to Portugal and Spain, which were to be my last stops on this trip. I decided to hitchhike from Northern Portugal to Barcelona. I arrived in Barcelona with only a few dollars, so the first thing I did was to go to an American Express office to see if my parents had sent me money. Luckily they had, and I also had the surprise of receiving a letter from a Cuban friend of mine. I was really surprised because he had no idea where I was, let alone that I would go to American Express. So I opened it and the only thing it said was, "Call me as soon as you receive this." For the life of me, I couldn't imagine why he might have written. Anyway, I called him thinking that maybe he had found a new job.

"Hello, hi, Stef! I thought you must not have received my note! Do you want to work for Bvlgari?"

"What?"

"You know, Bvlgari, the people I work for."

"No, I don't know a thing about jewelry."

"You don't have to. They'll teach you. They asked me a few weeks ago if I knew someone who spoke a few languages and who would make a good representative. I said no and then suddenly I remembered you and that besides Spanish, you also spoke some French and Portuguese, and that you were quite presentable. So I told them yesterday morning about you and they said, 'Bring him in,' and I said, I don't know where you are and they said, 'Find him!'"

So I flew back to Germany then went to Rome by train. I contacted them immediately, and they told me they would call me in few days. A week went by and I hadn't heard from them, so I called again and told them I had to leave soon. They said where to? They thought I lived in Rome and they invited me for lunch the next day. I accepted and that same afternoon I received a letter from home, with money, just in the nick of time because I only had left one pear and 35 cents.

I left for Germany the next evening, but since I needed to get back to start my new job, as soon as possible, I just went to the train station, where I had left most of my clothes, and returned to Rome. I was ready to start work in the most elegant place I had ever stepped foot in: Bvlgari.

I started to work in early November. Working hours were 930 to 1300 and then 1530 to1930, and everything was open when I was at work and closed when I was home. It was a very interesting job, and I loved both my new career and Roma, and besides, I felt very special as a Toma in Roma!

For the first three months in Italia, I went to the movies every day after work. It was my way of learning Italian because I was in an all-Italian atmosphere. Of course, I only went to see movies in Italiano and I sat in the front row and I stared at every speaker's mouth while they spoke. Also, the *fattorini*, the helpers, who worked at the store, befriended me, and I will always be grateful to this group of young men whose job was to stand next to the salesperson and as soon as he or she understood what the client wanted, he would tell the *fattorino*, "Please bring me the emerald earrings, or the ruby rings and the blue sapphire," somethings that he thought the client would like to see.

I became very close to most of them, and on the weekend a group of them always invited me to eat somewhere special or to see something special in the hills around Roma. And then one day an older woman who worked in the store called me aside and she began to give me a class in Roman society—

its good things and not-so-good things, and one of the not-so-good things was to hang around with the *fattorini*. No, this was a big mistake I was making! I should befriend the salespeople, not the helpers, who were of a lower class than the salespeople. This came as a big surprise to me. My answer to her sounded like it was practiced, but it wasn't. It was just shocking to hear her and I answered saying, "Madam, I think I understand you, but I don't agree. I'm not Italian, I'm American, and we usually befriend those who are nice to us, and the *fattorini* invite me several nights a week to see their homes and the weekend they invite me outside of the city to see the most beautiful things that the country has to offer. They make me feel as if I'm something special, and the other people who you want me to be closer to don't even give me the time of day. Some of them don't even say good morning to me."

Before I continue, I'll tell you about one of the many stories that could only have happened to me at my new working place. One day I was in the back of the store doing some midday resting and testing when one of the fattorini came looking for me.

"Signor Stefano, it's la Senora Taylor (Elizabeth), she's looking for you."

"For me? No, for Signor Gianni (Bvlgari). I told her, but, no, she asked for you. Hurry!"

"Hello, Miss Taylor! How are you today?"

"I'm fine, Sr. Toma. I'm leaving Rome and I just wanted to give you a Merry Christmas kiss!" We spoke for a few minutes and as soon as she walked out of the store, I was on the phone with Arizona, "Hi, Mom, you'll never guess . . ."

Today I again decided to write my memoirs because I had just been questioned for some major robberies that we had recently had. It was an exceptional day for various reasons: first, I was in Montreal, where, two, I applied for a visa to visit Cuba, and three, I fell in love with the ballet. I had attended a midday session at the theater, which explained the movements common to ballet, modern dance, or jazz. I learned that the movements in ballet can be compared with the same dimensions as voice, for example:

1. When listening to a conversation = you walk or march as normal
2. When listening to a more argumentative conversation = you march more theatrically and with gestures
3. If you insinuate certain "dimensions" = you use the body and certain dance steps

It was a very nice experience!

Here, I would like to mention again how much I appreciated the young men who I worked with in Italy. I have never been treated so well by a group of people in my life. It is because of them that I loved Italy so much. Without them I would not have understood the country so well, and I definitely would not have learned to speak Italian half as well as I could (at one time).

And it seemed strange to me that my new clients in New York City occasionally would invite me for a drink after work so I could get to know them. This was something that never happened in Italy.

CHAPTER 13

Danny and Rory, a Couple of Nephews

AFTER I HAD worked in the jewelry business for a while, I decided that I had to take my two nephews to Rome. I missed them so much and I was sure that they would like Rome, so I got permission to take them for a couple of weeks and since I was working in NYC again, I had my sister-in-law bring them to NY and we would leave from there. (They were ages eleven and seven.) I had spoken to the mother of a friend of mine, who had agreed to take care of them. However, she called me the morning we were supposed to leave to tell me that she was sick and could not take care of the children!

"Anita! Go to the Italian consulate and see if you can get a visa for Italy, today!" To make a long story short, she went to the consulate and the four of us were at the airport on time and arrived in Rome the next morning. Luckily, I had found a very inexpensive studio while I was learning the trade, and I still had it, so we were at home. You cannot imagine what it's like to be a kid from Phoenix, Arizona, let alone an uncle from Phoenix, Arizona, via Gary, Indiana, and have the opportunity to walk the streets, le strade di Roma, and no one knew we were a bunch of Tomas. Piazza Navona, pasta carbonara, non parliamo Italiano (sauf el tio). I want to try the champagne. How did you like it? Sciffoso, Piazza di Spagna, etc., etc., etc.

We also spent time together in Switzerland and Mexico. I worked for Marina B (Bvlgari) for the summer, so I had them stay with me the entire summer, plus we went to Mexico a couple of times together (it was closer). During the summer they spent it in Geneva. They both took French classes from 9 to 12 daily, and every single afternoon they went to a different museum. And they did this all summer and they never complained. Whenever they wanted to eat out, we ate out, under one condition—they had to order themselves, IN FRENCH!

Bvlgari was run by three brothers and two sisters who were cousins. At least that's how I remember it! Anyway, I was in Rome for a few weeks the summer after I left them, and I was asked if I would please go see Marina B who had recently opened a boutique in Geneva, named Marina B. I was very impressed with her, and lo and behold, she offered me a job! I thanked her profusely but declined because I was planning on going back to school. She asked me why, what did I want to get out of it. We talked about it quite a bit, and a few days later I arrived in Geneva to take up a new job. I worked for several months, and she asked me if I would go to London to open her shop there. I agreed but wasn't excited about it at all. Eventually and probably too soon, I decided to go back to school and to the mall, that's all, and after that I had a ball.

Our first trip to Mexico didn't go as smoothly as we imagined. We left from Nogales, Mexico, and we were supposed to arrive in the morning in Mazatlan, but we sat in the train for hours before we left. Then when we finally arrived, it was announced that we would leave in the evening, but that we would have to stay on the train because as soon as the train was fixed, it would leave. They finally let us get off to go swimming, but we stayed all night on the train, and we didn't sleep because we were waiting and waiting and waiting to leave. Finally we left and after a few more hours, they announced our next arrivals, including Guadalajara, where we were supposed to spend the day, but instead we continued straight to Mexico City.

We were lucky because none of us got too sick, that is to say that all three of us had stomach problems for about two days apiece during our first week in Mexico, but it never got any worse than having to make sure you knew where the closest bathroom was, and if I remember well, we all had it at the same time. But this is getting ahead of myself.

Being in Mexico with them was like magic for all of us. Of course we concentrated on seeing the main tourist sites, and they especially enjoyed going to see the Ballet Folklorico. I was sure they would be bored to death, but they didn't take their eyes off of it, *ni un secondo*. From Mexico City I took them to Monterey, where I left them with friends of mine—you know them, Mayu and Ricardo, they had two children almost of the same ages. I was hoping my nephews would learn Spanish, but I had no idea how it would work. However, they stayed about six weeks before I picked them up to take them home. And I called them once a week, which was something I'll never forget!

The first week I asked them, "Como va el Español?" They both answered, "What?" The second week they said, "Bien." By the time I went back to pick them up (about six weeks later), they were both speaking Spanish "quite decently." As a matter of fact when I picked them up, I again asked them "Como va el Español?" and one of them said, "El Castellano va bien," and the other said, "El Espanol no va bien pero el Mexicano, si, va bien. Do YOU understand?" ("How's your Spanish?" and one of them said, "Our Castilian is coming along well," and the other one said, "Our Spanish isn't coming along well, but our Mexican is.")

Between jobs and trips and school, I worked in Palm Beach one winter. I wanted to take it easy a little, and I was lucky again and I went to work with Van Cleef and Arpels, just for the winter season. Winter there is not winter in the normal sense of the word. People flock down to Florida, but I didn't do as well as I thought I would. I actually felt bad working for another jeweler. The one story I would like to tell here is that one evening I went to dinner with a group of ladies, one of which had just come back from southern Argentina, where she had gone to see the whales, and I remember her saying how important it was to save them and how you had to quit fishing the area as a start! She was about fifty years ahead of most everyone. It's a normal thing to hear today.

One other thing from this area that scared me to death was that I was staying for a weekend with a client, and about 3:00 in the morning, someone knocked on my door and said to grab everything I needed because we had to leave and they would explain later! Within five minutes, we were in the car on our way to the airport, so I was told. I didn't know where we were going because I knew where the airport was, more or less, and this was not the way. Finally, we drove on to a runway and within minutes, we were in the air. Then I understood that they would drop me off in Atlanta, which they did. I remember walking into a terminal where I purchased a ticket to NYC and then waited for either my flight or to be arrested, but for what, I still don't know.

STEFAN TOMA

CHAPTER 14

Preparing for the Second Half of My Life

WHEN I FINISHED writing my thesis, I asked my father if he would like to read it. Of course he would read it, and he made only one comment: "Not bad for a jeweler." Oh well, isn't this what most fathers would have said?

(Now let me see where exactly is TChad.)

In the early eighties, I went to live at home again with my parents and to work on a second master's or a doctorate. Everyone warned me not to work toward a doctorate as it would complicate my chances of working. Yes, eventually I would find something, but it would be much harder to find it because it would demand much higher wages.

Our neighbors had always made a big deal of my returning home. They said as soon as we returned from a trip that was any longer than a one day, I visited every tree in our yard to check it out and to see what was new! Anyway, I decided I wanted to study something that had to do with agriculture, so I worked toward a second master's, but this time in agricultural development, and I loved it! As a matter of fact it was the first time I can say that I really loved school. I even loved going to my classes and arriving at the university at 6 to 6:30 every morning. After a few weeks, I began to sit at the same table each day. At that time of the day, most of the students sitting at the table were Latin Americans, and soon I became a regular and I made several friends.

One of them was a student half my age, Gabriel, but we seemed to be on the same wavelength from our first meeting. He was from Mexico, and he was the first friend I made in my new career (or just prior to it). I'm sure we would be great friends if we lived closer to each other. As it was, I've only seen him at my wedding and then briefly in Dubai and Geneva.

I decided I would like to do some volunteer work, and eventually I found a part-time job, as a volunteer, at Food for the Hungry. One of my colleagues was going to be sent with his family in a few months to Latin America, and he asked me if I could teach him conversational Spanish in two or three months' time. I said I'd try. I had recently taken a Greek course, and I had enjoyed so much the teacher and his way of teaching that I decided to try to see if I could teach Spanish with the same gusto and love . . . and voila, it worked. And I must say I was surprised how well he handled the language. Before the gentleman left, he asked me—or I asked him, I don't remember which—if he could arrange an interview for me to work full-time for a nonprofit organization. A few weeks later, I flew to Southern California to talk to the people at World Vision. The interview went well, and a few weeks later I was offered a job. I was given the choice to go to either Tchad, or the Sudan. I had never imagined going to Africa, except I did wish to visit the Sudan to see this country that could be the breadbasket of Africa and the Middle East, so I eagerly accepted the post in Sudan. The last thing they told me was that they would call me in a short time, and that in the meanwhile I should make sure I had an up-to-date passport and vaccinations. Within a few days I was ready, and a week passed and then two and nearly a month had passed when I decided to call them. Oh, they said, the Sudan was not taking any new NGO staff and they understood that I wanted to go to the Sudan.

"Well, if you remember, I said that I would go anywhere, and you said that you needed people in both Tchad and the Sudan, and I repeated that it didn't make any difference and you repeated, Which one would you prefer. At that point I said would love to go to the Sudan, but if they are not taking people in the Sudan, I would love to go to Tchad." (Wherever that is.)

"Okay, we'll call you in a couple of days."

"Thank you very much, and remember that I don't mind where I go."

Well, to make a long story short, they called back in two days—it was Friday—and they asked me if I could leave that coming Monday. "Since you had me wait nearly a month, would you mind if I spend Christmas and New Year's with my family and I arrive there within two weeks?"

No, they said, they wouldn't mind at all, so I arrived in N'Djamena on the fifth of January 1986.

CHAPTER 15

A Couple of African Cities, N'Djamena and Maputo

WHAT A CHANGE in life! I was now living in a town of around three hundred thousand people and a country that had only about forty kilometers of paved road. On the first day I met my staff, and three days later I became head of the office when the lady who had been in charge left to go home until our new boss arrived. She left at 2:00 in the morning, and I drove a car full of colleagues to the airport to wish her well. It was the first time that I had driven in Africa, and after I had dropped off everyone, I had to find my way home and I wasn't sure which way to go and I was driving quite slowly. I turned onto a big roundabout and suddenly three fellows with machine guns jumped in front of my car with their guns all aimed at me. I rolled down the window and understood that I was too close to their hut. I pulled away and kept going until I found where I was staying.

I soon became used to this because there were only about two flights a week and everyone would go to the airport because it was the only place you could go to see other expats (expatriates) and have a beer.

One of the first things I had to face was the new national head of office, a rather good-looking young man who had been hired by the young (and single) lady who had just left. He was the newest member of the team and the highest-ranking, which wasn't to the liking of many of the old-timers. I had a chance to see why he wasn't so popular early on when I heard him say to a cleaning boy, "give me your hand," and when the man put out his hand, he spit his gum into it, which is not exactly something that you do when you've become the head of office! In a couple of days, he was put at the level he should have been put in the first place.

One of the first trips I took was to Moundou in southern Tchad to see some of our projects there. We decided to drive instead of fly, and we left early in the morning and went across the river, by bridge, to a more developed country, Cameron, which had a paved road that we could drive on most of the way to Moundou. Between my passport, their passports, the checkpoints on the bridge, and the fact that someone had to go back to the office to pick up something, it was almost dark when we were finally ready to head south, so we decided to spend the night in the village on the other side of the river. We could see our office from our hotel. Anyway, we left early the next morning and by the late afternoon we were back in Tchad. In one of the places that we had to stop by (so they could check our passports, again), the man that was talking to us kept asking more questions and wanting to see every piece of paper we had in our briefcases and wallets. When we started to get a little short with him, he announced with a rather angered mood, "You know, I even have the right to tear up your letters!" The next time, we decided to fly down, and the only thing that was like the first trip was upon arriving at the airport, there was a soldier looking at our documents as we got off the plane. He went through them page by page, until he realized that they were upside down. Then he turned mine right side up, and after he had completely scrutinized it, he said to me, *"Vous etes quelle nationalite?"* ("What nationality are you?")

Just to give you an idea of what the city looked like, after I had been there a little while, I found out that a new ambassador arrived to take up his assignment. I don't remember from which country, but after the plane landed, he was whisked through customs and immigration and was taken to his new home, which was more than quite nice, but the road to get there must have turned him off because he didn't even take his things out of the car. He just went back to the airport, got back on the same flight that he arrived on, and decided not to assume his new assignment.

The city had a population of over three hundred thousand, about the same as Phoenix when I moved there, but this is a lousy comparison. N'Djamena didn't seem like a city; it was more like a couple hundred thousand people living together in the desert. It was a desert in the winter, dry, dry, dry, but in the summer it was wet, wet, wet, underwater. The wet season snuck up on you, and the first rain found every single N'Djamenois outside preparing the land. I'm not exaggerating, every store was closed because you had to take care of your crops on the first couple of days of the rainy season or forget it, and I do mean FORGET IT! It would dry up and you would be without veggies. For the rest of the rainy season, you have to drive very carefully because the roads are all underwater. All in all, you can't imagine how much I miss it!

I'll never forget my house; it was a modern European house in the middle of a behind-schedule fourth-world country. I got tired of fourth-world hotel life and I started to look for a house. Again, I was lucky because I found two of them and I eventually moved into one of them, and my boss, who arrived a couple of weeks after me, took the other one. Of course, a four-bedroom house was too much for me, but finding tenants was very easy. Two young ladies that I worked with immediately took a room, plus I had just hired a young man from Burkino Faso, Minkutu, for my agriculture projects. He was very easy to get along with and he was married and had a new son, so he was just the right person to take the third room and eventually one of the others. I also hired a young man to cook for us. He cooked quite well, although I could never recognize what he was making. One thing I cannot forget was the first time I asked him if he would make us some popcorn. He said he'd be happy to make it, and then about ten minutes later, he called me into the kitchen and said that he had no idea what to do with it. I said, "Oh, sorry, it's very easy. Just put about two or three spoons full of oil into the pot and about a cup full of popcorn," which I did. Then I covered the pot and put it on the fire. When it started to pop, I occasionally picked it up and shook it. When it quit popping, I took the lid off and it was completely filled with corn. If you could have seen the face on our cook, he looked at it in disbelief, grabbed the pot, and picked it up to inspect it to figure out how the popcorn got in. He had never seen such a thing before!

STEFAN TOMA

I had always thought that I would like to try out to be in a play, so when I saw an article saying that the Tchadian-American Theatre group was looking for people to fill the cast of their first play of the season. I decided to go for it. And what do you know, I got the leading role as the Prince of Nonomura in *Sheep on the Runway*. During the organizational meeting, I saw a very cute young lady who I thought was surely from Brooklyn. Her name was Rose and she became my prompter and later on something else. The play was a success, and I became quite close to her, no, very close! Just to give you an idea, today, she's still my prompter!

However, she wasn't too happy that I thought she was from Brooklyn. She was from a half a world away, from Lebanon, and her parents were from a bit closer, from Palestine. Lebanon, Palestine, Brooklyn, what's the difference? She was cute! Anyway, she had been working in New York before coming to Tchad, so the look must have rubbed off on her. And I was very happy to know that she was from the Middle East! We spent all our free time with each other, even after I found out where I would be going to be for the next two years.

After I was there a while, I became very close to all of the Tchadians that I worked with, plus it became normal to travel around the country with them. I loved it. After I was there a few months, I was told that I should go to back to Europe for a rest and a change of scenery. I decided to go to Paris, where I visited all of the jewelry shops. I found out that they were having a special Biennale de Bijouterie, a jewelry show which they have every two or three years. I bought a ticket and I immediately found many people that I knew from NY, Rome, and Geneva. I had such a good time that I was worried about how I was going to take living in N'Djamena again! Anyway, after a week, I went back, and I had no sooner arrived that I went to the office and I knew immediately that my jewelry days were over. I had chosen the right route!

I spent all of my free time with Rose, and much later on, I wrote this for the "Queens of N'Djamena," who were:

Carole, American;
Cecille, French and Spanish, now just called a European!;

Hedda, Finnish;
Kathleen, also American;
Pamela, English;
Philomene, Tchadienne;
Tanny, Dutch; and
Rose, Lebanese and also known as La Vrai Rose de N'Djamena.

There's a place called N'Djamena,
Not a place you see by bus
It's in the heart of Africa,
Quite well hidden from most of us

The travel guides don't mention it,
And no one makes a fuss,
It's not on many lists to visit,
So if you're not ready, you'll cuss it and not discuss it.

But don't pass it by too lightly,
You may someday want to go,
As did a group in the '80s,
To preach, to teach, and to sow!

It's in a place seemingly forgotten by God,
But when things again get tough,
Just spread your wings and go there,
As we haven't yet done enough

Now, to tell you a tiny story,
It's one that's not glad or sad,
It's about helping lovely people,
In a wonderful place called Tchad!

So read this book and go there
If you're inspired or not,

At any age, just be a volunteer
You can really do a lot.

By the way, this group of young women still gets together once a year for at least a long weekend. And when they're together, it's as if they're together with family for a Thanksgiving weekend.

Maputo

Come Christmas and everyone is ready to spend a few days at home, if they can. At the end of my second year, I left earlier than most of my friends, because I knew that I had a new assignment, Maputo! And I'm not cussing, no, that was my new assignment. After a nice Christmas, I was now on my way to one of the Portuguese-speaking countries in Africa. (Now, let me see exactly where is Tchad, I mean Mozambique!)

What a city! I arrived on the weekend, so I had time to walk the whole city, I thought! But I was wrong; it was only the touristic area. I stayed at a rather nice hotel, which helped me understand why I was sent. For one thing, they had no food, not only at the hotel but in the whole city. The Russians imported every fish that was caught. Notice that I did not say "that they caught." No, I said, "that was caught," period, into the Soviet Union. The only food that you could find in the markets was cabbage and carrots. And there were lots of nice-looking restaurants, but you couldn't get into them. And when you found one you could get into, it was mainly because there was no food left or that they had no food, period. Luckily, this lasted only about three weeks more. But at the time, I had no idea when it would end. I ate at a different place almost every night, until one night, I ate at a restaurant near the hotel that I hadn't been able to get into until that night, mainly because it was usually not even open. It was so nice and had a good menu, more or less. Much to my surprise, they had a small group that played music, and everyone who was eating also sang. I asked them before I left if they were going to be open the following night, and they said yes. Then I asked what they were going to have on the menu, and they said "the same thing." So I asked them if I could bring in seven or eight people, and they also said yes. Too many yeses. I wonder what's wrong.

The following day, everyone in my office accepted, but I don't think any of them thought that they would have a good time. Well, let me tell you, it was the beginning of the end of the saddest place I've seen, any place. The rest of my stay was wonderful, and I do mean wonderful. Even the problems I had turned out to be nothing. It was a beautiful country filled with beautiful things. I still have a couple of paintings.

My first trip was a short flight to a city I'd never heard of. We left at the end of the morning, and since it was a very small plane, I managed to be in the cockpit right before we landed. The pilot was speaking Portuguese and I had a hard time understanding him. Finally, I understood that we were going to fly over some government buildings and he wanted to know what color the flag was flying over them. I don't remember the color, but everyone cheered and we landed. Later on, I asked what the color of the flag meant. They said, "Oh! You don't know? If it was any other color, we wouldn't have landed." As it was, it was our flag, but if we had tried to land at an airport where the enemy had taken over, who knows what would happen, but it's not something that you could have written home about!

I met a very nice Russian lady who was married to a Mozambican. She was an artist, a painter, and her paintings, according to me, didn't have a drop of Russian blood. They were 100 percent Mozambican! I bought several of her paintings and through her, I met several other Mozambican painters, and that's when I started my painting collection. I bought several more of them, so I managed to keep a bit of Mozambique, Romania, Moldova, and other countries alive through their artwork.

STEFAN TOMA

CHAPTER 16

Afghanistan (First of a Couple of Visits) and *El Senor Me Escucho *(The Second of a Couple, Two or Three Times)

---◇---

O NE AFTERNOON, I was in the office working late when the phone rang.

"Stefan!" It was my boss calling from the States.

"How are you?" I said.

"Fine," he said. "Do you still have your beard?"

"Of course!"

"Good! You're going to use it!"

"Sorry, what did you say?"

"I said good, you're going to use it."

"What do you mean?"

"I mean you're going to use it, you're going to Afghanistan!"

And ten days later, I was on a flight taking me to Peshawar, where I was to live and travel back and forth to my new job in Afghanistan, replanting fruit trees that had been destroyed in the war. It was a wonderful project, and the people were so appreciative! Anyway, after a few weeks in Afghanistan, I was told to go back to Peshawar for a rest. Since I had a whole week, I decided to take a bus trip up to the Chinese border. It was a very easy trip. We travelled by bus for two days, stopping at interesting villages and tourist sites, until we arrived at the border, "Voila, la Chine," and we left to return to Peshawar. When we were a few hours from Peshawar, I called my office and found out that my right-hand man in Afghanistan had been shot by mistake. When I arrived a few hours later, I found out all of the details. Anyway to make a long story a bit shorter (2MALSS), his roommate was playing with a gun, which was thought to be empty and it wasn't! So it was decided that we should go to his home in a mountain village to tell his father. And the only person that the whole office would accept to replace him was his brother who was in Switzerland, whom I managed to get back to Afghanistan in a very short time and who definitely did not want his brother's job. But we all left, including the brother, in a minibus for his father's village.

That morning before we got on the bus, I prayed! Please, dear God, take care of us! Now, we were on the bus where everyone was arguing and yelling. There were not too many cars on the road, but every time one went by us, everyone stuck their head out the window to see better who was in the other vehicle. I closed my eyes for a minute and again said, "Please, God, I need to feel your presence!" Suddenly, and I know this is hard to believe, I felt HIS HAND on my shoulder! And I still remember it when I tell this story. We arrived at his father's house where we sat for two days, during which people came by in small groups, nonstop. When each person, family, or group arrived, they said a quick (or a not-so-quick) prayer and said something nice about him. Besides the time this took, they also translated, more or less, everything to me. And I wasn't scared at all! Well, a little.

CHAPTER 17

Romania Schools

IN APRIL, I arrived for my next two-year assignment in, would you believe it, in Romania. It was a dream come true. My grandparents and four aunts and uncles were born there (My father and three other aunts and uncles were born in the US). Unfortunately, I knew very little Romanian. I arrived a couple of days before my birthday. I didn't know a soul. I think I had one or two names of people I could contact that might be able to help me.

I started to put together a small office. One of the first people I hired was a young lady, Michaela, who not only knew how to work on a computer, but she had also built her computer, almost from scratch, using a television she had found. Then, and I don't remember how I found it, but I found a nice, rather large house in the middle of Bucharest. I eventually moved in and slept in the office, but it worked quite well, unless I got up late!

The first few weeks, I stayed in a hotel, but I finally decided to stay in the office. For the first few weeks, I went every night to Piata Universitatii to watch the protesting. At the end of the first week, I found a young man, or he found me, I don't remember which, but anyway, he was there every night, his English was pretty good, and he kept me up with what was happening, and there was a lot happening! In a very short time, we started to work. We had a truckload of medicine come and we had several hospitals that needed everything we had. So we took the first container of medicine and medical equipment to Iasi. I didn't have anyone yet who could travel, so I asked the fellow whom I saw every night at Piata Universitatii, Ionut, if he would like to come to work with me. And I liked his answer.

He said, "Can you come to my house and explain to my parents what we will be doing?"

"Of course, I would love to tell your parents about your work and about World Vision, in general. Let's go!"

So we went, and in a few days we were on the road. Everything was going well and we had a full-fledged World Vision office working. I would just like to say here that Ionut, John, has now worked for many years for the Cleveland Clinic, and he and his wife, Roxanna, who also worked for World Vision, are still best friends with me.

One of the things I'd like to say about Romanians is that you cannot tell by the way they act in public how friendly they are going to be. The generation that I was getting to know grew up in a very communistic, do this, do that regime. So, again, just 2MLSS, the first week, I was walking back to the hotel and an older Romanian angrily yelled at me. He sounded like he was telling me off, so I said, "'Cum' what?"

And he said again in a little better accent, "You look like you're enjoying yourself, keep it up."

Why couldn't he have said it the first time with that nice sound in his voice? The first time, he sounded like he was really pissed off with something I was doing wrong, at least in his eyes. Many of my friends didn't seem like they'd ever be my friends when I first met them.

Another thing is that I don't think that any normal citizen knew what was going on. I was told that there were over one hundred thousand abandoned children and I'm sure it was true. Not only did I visit the institutes where they were found, my hotel was like a bazaar for buying little kids. It was UN, and I do mean UNBELIEVABLE. I would see someone one night and the next night they would have three or four children, of which they were planning to take two of them home and just showing the others off to the other foreigners!

Other very strange things were the "homes for the irrecoverables." They were filled with bright people who wrote, painted, and made things that were beautiful. I talked to some of them (through an interpreter) and found out that some of them were so very bright that I guess that is why they were considered irrecoverable!

STEFAN TOMA

CHAPTER 18

*El Senor Me Escucho (Third Time) and Me Hablo (First Time) *Our Father Listened to Me and Spoke to Me

ONE DAY, I received a letter from Rose saying that she was flying to Montreal in a few weeks via Paris and she wondered if I would be able to go to Paris for a few days. I immediately decided to go, but then I found out that I had too much to do that had to be done right away, so I couldn't go. Then I called her and asked her if she couldn't come to Bucharest. She said that she would let me know in a few days if there were any possibilities. These few days seemed like a month, but she phoned me back with dates and everything changed. I was so excited with the possibility of seeing her again that I started planning. That night, before I went to bed, I grabbed my Bible and I said, "OK, God, tell me something about this trip!" I placed my finger on an unknown page and started to read. It was the first time you spoke to me! And it was very direct. My finger was on Genesis? No! Salmos? Uh, no! Luc? To tell you the truth, I don't remember. The only thing I remember was that it said something that had something to do with *matrimonio*, getting married. So I had that in my mind! Well, let's see!

CHAPTER 19

I Like the Middle East

WHY DO MY days in the Middle East remain so sweet in my memory? I feel at home most anywhere in the area, but especially in Syria, Lebanon, and Egypt. Could it be because I like a certain flower from there? (*"Sera que me gusta una cierta flor de ahi?"*)

The trouble that I have now is that my children, before they were eighteen, lived in five different countries that all spoke different languages. Now that they feel at home in Canada, they are adamant to make it their home. They've both done well and have become very Canadian and are great Quebecois citizens. So, for the time being, don't ask them to work in a foreign country unless it's North America, which is foreign but not too much. Anyway, for the time being, they would rather live in North America. When things get better, maybe we'll spend a few months each year in one of the Eastern countries, but if not . . . well, it was nice.

A few weeks passed and Rose arrived in Romania. I had a lot of things to show her as well as a lot of things to tell her, and I think she felt it. So on the second day, we were in a beautiful park and we were having a very good time. Then she suddenly said, "Stef, why don't we get married?"

"Let's do," I immediately said.

And that was it. After that, that's all we talked about.

Of course, she eventually asked me a very important question: "What church shall we be married in?"

"The Orthodox Church, of course," I said.

"No, you can't get married in the Orthodox Church unless you're Orthodox. And you're not!"

"Don't worry," I said, "I will be by the time we get married!"

She left for Canada a few days later.

CHAPTER 20

Northern Romania, a Letter

August 1991
Iasi, Romania

Iubita Rose,

MONDAY WAS ONE of those rare days in life when everything that happened seemed to be predestined, timed by the cosmos. On Saturday, I learned that the Metropolitan of Moldova and Bucovina would see me on Monday at noon. Rather than stand by for a flight on Monday morning and possibly miss such an extraordinary encounter, I decided to go to Iasi on Sunday night. Alexandru and Steriana accompanied me to the train station around 1600, and at 1715, I departed. At 2315, I arrived at the station in Iasi and walked to the hotel where I normally stay.

In the morning, I went directly to the orphanage where part of our team was working to meet the people who had helped arrange the meeting. I was told that I was to meet with Metropolitan Daniel Ciobotea at 1000 and then I would return to the church between 1200 and 1300 for the ceremony. A friend and WV staff member, John Bratoloveano, accompanied me to the Metropolia and we arrived promptly at 1000. Soon after our arrival, we were greeted by Daniel, who spoke with us and exchanged pleasantries for about an hour before I was introduced to my spiritual guide, Ieronim Clement Hamalan. Clement's first impression on me was one of a very stern, possibly dangerous churchling. I then went off with him for approximately one and a half hours on my voyage of learning and confessing past sins for a spiritual renaissance and preparation for our wedding. I was so happy, I felt like a child. After all this and learning about the morning and evening prayer schedule, how to pray, how to kneel properly (crossing of oneself and learning *"in numele tatalui, fiului, si duhului sfint,"* (in the name of the Father, Son, and Holy Spirit) and several other acts, the equivalent of the salaat and bi ism allahs I'd heard in many a neighbour), Father Daniel appeared again, embraced me, and began the liturgy for my anointment. I read a statement of faith filled with several words which I still need to more closely define, prayed, was prayed for, kissed several icons which somewhere in the backwaters of my mind another voice prayed that God had zapped any germs which might have been put there by the enemy, generally bubbled inside, and was put on a spiritual cloud on which I'm still traveling on. Finally, I received another embrace from Father Daniel, followed by the same from my witnesses, Olimpia Macovei and Dr. Ciongradi. My brother, Clement, suddenly seemed like a lifelong friend. I had his coordinates, so that when in spiritual panne (Breakdown), I could ring him for any type of confidence. Daniel gave me a book in English and several others in Romanian regarding the church. He also gave me a rustic beautiful cross contained in a small closable box which I can carry with me in my travels. We then retired to the building of the Metropolitan, where we had cake and wine and learned of the coup d ètat that was taking place at a neighboring country about ten miles up the road. (This was a revolution staged by the Russians. They took part of Romania, which, about fifty years later, that would be today, became the Moldovan Republic.) That was how I passed Monday, the 19th of August, 1991. Cu dragoste, te quiero.

CHAPTER 21

A Couple of Moms:
Hello, Madame Awad, Hi,
Mom, Guess What?

⁂

A COUPLE OF days after we decided, Rose left and I decided that it was time to call her mother. Rose had suggested that I didn't call her until she was about to arrive, because such news would be hard to digest if she didn't have the whole story! So I was waiting to hear her voice and to ask her if she would give me her permission to marry her daughter. Unfortunately, she couldn't understand me and then the line fell, and her daughter had not yet arrived so she did not know who I was and even worse, what I was trying to tell her. She just knew that it had something to do with her daughter! I also called my mother.

Still Chapter 21: Hi, Ma, Guess What?

I said, "Guess what, Mom, I'm getting married. And we've decided to have the ceremony at a church in Montreal on the 15th of September, so we would like to come home the week before so we can celebrate your anniversary and then come together to Montreal."

"That's fine! Come as soon as you can and we'll work things out."
So we arrived and one of the first things my father said to her was, "So, Rose, what would you like to do while you're here?"

"Whatever you decide is all right with me," she said.

"Would you like to go to Las Vegas?" he asked.

"Oh, oh my God, yes, I'd love to do that," she said.

So we left. There were seven people in the car: my mom and dad, my cousin Barbara and her husband, my sister-in-law, and Rose and I (My brother couldn't go. He had to work). It was a great trip, and we all got to know each other. After we returned, we celebrated Mom and Dad's fiftieth anniversary and then we all left for Montreal. The night before we left, we had dinner at Green Gables, one of my favorite restaurants in the Valley of the Sun, and then went to a park where we rented a gondola for a couple of hours. And since I had plenty to drink at dinner and I was in a rare mood, I not only paddled but sang, to the amazement of the other *gondoleros*. It was a wonderfully great evening and we left the next day for Montreal (including bro).

We had looked at several places that would have made beautiful backgrounds for our wedding; four in particular stood out:

1. Beirut; however, America and Lebanon didn't have diplomatic relations, so forget it, I mean the groom would have to stay home.
2. Bucharest; however, it's too far away and too remote for most of our guests, so we'll forget it also.
3. Phoenix, would have been nice; however, it would be too hot (around 100) for many of our guests, especially the older ones.
4. So we decided on Montreal, and it was probably the best place because many of Rose's relatives had recently moved there, including her mother, two sisters, and her brother, plus many, many cousins, aunts, and uncles. I also had quite a few cousins who didn't live too far away.

The wedding was gorgeous, if I must say so myself. Afterward, we left in the limousine to have our pictures taken. Then on the way back to the hotel where we were having an evening of festivities, we stopped at a McDonald's and had a snack (you'd think people had never seen a bride and groom before!). Then it was back to the hotel for the festivities. It was a great evening. We had dinner and then danced the night away. It was one of the few times that both of our families were together. (I recently saw the film and it was even more fun than I had remembered!) The next evening, we left for Europe, where we had a very short honeymoon in Italy, which was still my favorite European country. We, of course, went to see all of the places I had become attached to, starting with Piazza di Spagna and Via Condotti (the street of Bvlgari), Via Vittoria (the street where I lived), Piazza del Popolo, Piazza Navona, and last but definitely not the least, Piazza del Vaticano. And it seems like we had about as much time as it took me to write the names of the places I just mentioned.

Then I went back to Bucharest and Rose went back to N'Djamena to find out where she was going to be sent on her next assignment, which we didn't know yet. Basically, we both liked our jobs. She was working for the United Nations and she knew that she was due for a new assignment any day. A few weeks passed and I was kept busy with our projects, especially those that we were doing together with the U.S. and the UN. We had some really dedicated young ladies working in a clinic on the coast with children with AIDS. It was one of the hardest-hit areas for the first pandemic that I remember.

CHAPTER 22

Oman (Our First Stay Together), Afghanistan (Second Stay, But Not Together)

WHEN SHE FINALLY announced that she'd be leaving in a few weeks for her new assignment, I couldn't wait to know any longer where my new home would be. We had decided that I would probably leave my job and look for something in Rose's new area if we both were in agreement. Where is it going to be? I'm dying to know!

Oman? That's great. Maybe I can learn Arabic! Then I started to worry about all sorts of things. First of all, the cost of moving. Second, what jobs might be available? Oh yeah, where is it? When should I tell my boss? And how, because he's really been good to me. Anyway, I'm sure that she'll feel well there. *So don't worry*, I said to myself, *you have time before you have to leave.* Well, 2MLSS, I finally left hot and cold Romania for hot and hot Oman. (Romania was hot because I loved it and cold because it was cold, and Oman was hot because I loved why I was going there and hot because it was hot, very!

I loved it. It was the nicest place you could imagine. The houses all looked as though they'd just been painted, the cars were all clean, and people were very nice and very polite. Just to give you an idea, well two: The first is just hearsay, and that is you had to keep your car clean; otherwise, you would be stopped by the police, who wouldn't yell at you or anything like that, no—"Hello" or "good afternoon." "I am sorry to stop you, but please, while you're in Oman, try to keep your car a little more tidy."

Rose and I went to the beach several days a week, almost always to the same one, which was close to where we lived. One day, we met a young man who eventually became a good friend of ours; however, when Rose went to the beach by herself, or before me, he never spoke to her unless I was there. Now, if that's not being polite. Eventually, he came with his wife, who swam with us, although she was fully dressed, it seemed. And we will never forget the beach. It was about a mile from our house, the water was crystal clear, and every time we went, we saw different types of animals in the water: turtles of all sizes, squid, and millions of fish. And not to mention I felt like I was in the Bible, because as I was swimming, I would, all of a sudden, find myself in front of a wall of fish and they would part and let me go through the crystal-like water, and I felt that the sea was parting for me!

We spent a lot of our time with an Egyptian family. Samir and Mona had five children and we dedicated a lot of time to their two teenagers. They were more like cousins than simply friends. Language-wise, it was quite interesting because when they spoke to Rose, they spoke Arabic, and when they were talking to me, they tried to speak English, so we were always hearing both languages, but it didn't do me much good.

I was lucky that I worked the first month I was there, but afterward I couldn't find anything. Then one day, the telephone rang and it was the UN enquiring if I would like, or better said if I would be willing to go back to Afghanistan. I said, "Yes," but could I let them know for sure tomorrow.

They said, "Yes, of course."

So Rose and I decided together that I should go and who knows, maybe I would eventually join the UN, eventually. About a week later, I left for Herat and I must say, it was a nice place, but it didn't last. Rose took advantage of my next leave, which was exactly at Christmas. We were getting ready to return to our assigned areas on the second or third of January when I heard that a war had started and it was too dangerous to FLY back to Herat. After five or six days, I was notified that it would behoove me to go to Jalalabad, where I was to coordinate the work of the various UN organizations, plus if I could help find an area where we could put families that had lost their homes in the capital. I was asked to go until they found someone who could take over and I could go back to Herat. I really was too busy to think! In the morning, I oversaw the arrival of the families who were arriving from Kabul, and in the afternoon, from around 16:00 on, all of the UN agencies would meet and each organization would tell all the others what they had done that day and what they planned to do the next day. I was really a fast typist then, so as we spoke, I took everything down. Then I went back to my room, corrected the document, and sent it to our office in Jalalabad. Four months went by and I was really pooped from all of the various jobs I had undertaken. Things had slowed down a bit and I was given permission to go back to Herat, where I was involved in coordination but not the head of it. My main responsibility was to take care of the UN house, which I enjoyed very much. I was always being asked by the kitchen staff what they should make, so I started telling them how to cook. Luckily, I had a decent idea of how to make various dishes, and when I left, the three things I was very happy with was that I got along with everyone on both sides, Afghans and all of the UN workers, I taught the various UN groups to play progressive gin, which had everyone participating and at the same time discussing what they had to do the next day, plus I had been carrying out "Cultural Tuesdays," where we had a specific dinner, such as Mexican food, Italian food, or other people's food with a film that matched it, so we had a Mexican movie the night we had Mexican food, a French movie the night we had French food, etc.

One thing I forgot to *mention, when we went to the market in Peshawar, she had to cover her face like the local women did. The first time we went, she didn't cover herself well and I can't believe how the men stared at her, practically nose to nose!*

I went back to Oman at least once a month. I started applying for assignments and I was eventually asked to go to New York (via Geneva) for an interview with UNICEF for Georgia. Just before I was finished with the interview, I was asked if I spoke Romanian. I said, "Yes, but not fluently."

They said, "We are going to have a place for someone in Moldova, would that interest you?"

"Yes," I said with a big smile on my face.

"And where would you rather go, to Georgia or Moldova?"

What a question. Of course, if I had to make a choice, I would choose Moldova, but I answered them, "It makes no difference. I would love to go to either place."

CHAPTER 23

Chisinau, a Couple of Kids

A COUPLE OF weeks went by and I received a letter from them thanking me for my interest, but they had chosen another candidate. I immediately sat down and wrote them a letter applying for the position in Moldova, and what do you know, I was soon on my way to Chisinau, where I spent the happiest days of my life. Rose arrived soon after and her Romanian is good, maybe even better than mine. We had two children who are both about to finish university, plus we made several lifelong friends. In all, we were there nearly six years, amen, more than any other place. I didn't realize it for a couple of years, but as I've already said, Moldova had become the Moldovan Republic the day I became Orthodox!

We had both of our children in Moldova. It was interesting to watch them adapt to different people and situations. For example, language: I spoke to my son the first year in Spanish, but I switched to English because I didn't speak to anyone else in Spanish, so the first languages of both my son and daughter were English, Arabic, and Romanian, which they were completely at ease with until we were assigned to an Arabic-speaking region. And that was that; after a few months, not a word more of Romanian came out of their mouths. I take that back, two Romanian words were still heard from all of us: Ticalos and Nebuna, Nasty and Crazy; these were the names of our two cats that we had brought from Oman. I always felt strange when I had to call them. I mean, imagine hearing someone in the street yelling, "Oh, Crazy, where are you? Come on, Nasty, come home!" Anyway, neither of the children speaks Romanian, but both of them are at home with English, French, and to a less extent, Arabic.

I started out working in the basement of the UN in Chisinau. After I hired the first few staff members, we moved into our own quarters. The first new staff members were already working for the UN, so they were used to speaking Russian. As I mentioned, Moldova had been part of the Soviet Union for several decades, so everyone spoke Russki in public as well as in the office because the educational system had been in Russian up until Moldova won its independence in 1991. Anyway, the combination of Russian and Romanian must have been a good one because *I soon had an office of bright bilingual Moldovans, or should I say, multilingual Moldovans. Twenty years later, most of my office still works for UNICEF, or the UN, but internationally. Among them, I still hear from Octavian, Larissa, Igor, Elena, and Violeta, who, by the way, are multilingual because they all speak Russian, Romanian, French, or another language, and English. We lived in a small duplex that we shared with Romanian speakers, which greatly helped our language learning. My wife used to complain after she went to the big market place because she would order in Romanian and they would answer in Russian, and neither of us spoke even a little Russian. However "Chisinau" has become like a magic word in our household. One more thing I'd like to mention about Chisinau, pronounced like "quishi-now," is that we became Moldovans ourselves. And after I settled in, every other Thursday, we ate out at a different restaurant. Everyone in the office who was up to it went and we split the bill.*

CHAPTER 24

Riyadh and Geneva, the Last Couple of Places Where I Worked

MY LAST ASSIGNMENT was in Riyadh, Saudi Arabia, but I was also in charge of UNICEF in the United Arab Emirates, Qatar, Bahrain, and Kuwait. I enjoyed my stay, although now when I think back, I feel that I could have done better, much better! Anyway, we enrolled the children in a French school in case we decided to go back to the city where we married. I was eventually sent out of the country because there was a killing spree going on against Westerners. I finished the last days of my career in Geneva, where my wife went back to work for the UN, to be exact UNAIDS, and the children went to school in French and became ready to settle down in Canada. Life in Geneva was very nice. We found a very beautiful house in the mountains, where we stayed until we decided to move to Geneva City, where we were closer to Rose's office. I believe now that for the children, it was the best place we lived and the best place we could live.

CHAPTER 25

Cairo and Montreal, the Last Couple of Places We Lived in, So Far!

EGYPT WAS LIKE going home, mainly because we had friends there, the same ones we had in Oman. The main difference was that the five kids were no longer little kids. No, now they were all married, big kids with little kids. And our kids were no longer little either!

We lived in Cairo, but we adopted Dahab as our favorite place to spend a weekend or even a day. There were a lot of art galleries, where we bought several paintings. Unfortunately, I absolutely have no space to hang another one, well maybe one!

Also, one of my best friends, Mohsen, from graduate school was from Egypt, but he wasn't there all of the time. Anyway, with our Egyptian friends from Oman, we felt like we were at home. Toward the end of 2017, my wife decided to take early retirement, so we are all in Montreal now.

Our son and daughter didn't feel at home in Egypt, probably because of the Arabic, which they were beginning to understand and speak better but couldn't read it at all. Also, our daughter, who was becoming a beautiful teenager, couldn't go out without drawing the attention of all the teenage boys in the area, so she went to live with her aunts in Montreal, where she graduated from high school. Our son was already in his last year of high school and he graduated from an English high school in Cairo and then graduated from a university in Ottawa. And we love them both and there is no way of saying how much!

Have I lived here in Montreal all of my life? If so, that means I have quite an imagination! I mean, how could I imagine what it was like to be born in Gary, Indiana, and then to live, or maybe I should say to stay in, if only for a short time, in places like Aleppo, Bahrain, Beirut, Bogota, Bucharest, Budapest, Buenos Aires, Cairo, Chisinau, Damascus, Dubai, Fayetteville, Geneva, Iasi, Kuwait City, London, Managua, Mexico City, Miami, Montreal, New York, Oxford, Palm Beach, Phoenix, Qatar, Riyadh, Rome, Roseburg, San Juan, Scottsdale, Venice, ETC. I can't tell you which of these cities I liked the best because I loved them all at one time, but maybe Chisinau, Rome, Cairo, Montreal, and Beirut are among the tops, and let's not forget, of course, my favorite city of fifty years ago, Damascus!

LAST CHAPTER

WELL, IT'S NOT a long story and I probably could write a sequel, but I don't think I have the energy. So instead, here's a poem I wrote that brings things up to date, at least until the twenty-first of the month (March), the day I get vaccinated. It's called Corona...(Please excuse anything you don't understand from here on in, I probably don't understand it either!)

CORONA

Why are the streets so empty, I ASK/. And why are people wearing something blue or black? Oh, a MASK!
I don't have anything and I'm getting kinda OLD/. So if I come down with something, I'm gonna have to be BOLD!
So I guess I will have to wear one TOO/, at least that's what I've been told I should DO!
Could it be that everyone is on VACATION/? If so, tell me, please, just what is their VOCATION!
Come to think of it, you haven't been by to see me at my STATION/, so then it must be the whole NATION!
Why are the streets so empty. Oh I KNOW/. I guess at this time of the year, we were waiting for a little SNOW!
Well, speak all you want, really, if you MUST/. Anyway, be glad it's snow, so don't bite the DUST!
Now you can really do as you PLEASE/, but don't get too close and for God's sake, don't SNEEZE!

And why aren't there more people in the STORE/? I haven't the slightest.
Do we really need many MORE?

And we're not able to go out, but what the HECK/. There's plenty to
do at home here in QUEBEC!

(Il y a beaucoup a faire dan les maisons ici a QUEBEC!)

Now, where are people, have they left or been TAKEN/? Don't know.
Maybe they're hidden and FAKING!

And why is that president (Trump) making such a FUSS/? He doesn't
realize he's talking to all of US!

And down on the border, why keep some people OUT/? Don't yell at
them, please, and don't SHOUT!

And if a Mexican says, "Una Corona," please do not SCREAM/. He
doesn't want a mold; maybe a beer or just an ice CREAM!

Why are the streets so empty? I'll tell you WHY/, and believe me, I can
tell you no LIE!

God above is looking down on US/. He knows what has to be done, so
don't make such a FUSS!

Now, we can see the other side of this STREET/. And the rest he'll leave
to us, until we finally MEET!

I dedicate this to Elias, Rose's cousin, and to all of you, you, brother,
sister, father, mother, cousin, and others who we passed the CORONA
time with, especially Amalia, Rami, Rodrigo, Esteban, Rory, Danny,
Fuad, Marya, Pavley, Pauline, and Peter!

HOW TO CHANGE THE WORLD TO YOUR LIKING, SLOWLY BUT SURELY, COULD WE AND SHOULD WE, WE SHOULD

Could we think about solving our problems through LOVE?
If we could do it as if we're talking to those of us who are already ABOVE!

If we could do so and be sure our thoughts are free from EVIL,
And be sure nothing comes from the devil, that evil WEAVIL.

I'm sure that we can change things here on EARTH
But it will have to be more than just a dearth of the EARTH.

We will have to start thinking like this TODAY,
Why wait, we can't wait, there is no other WAY!

We have to start by thinking of us ALL,
I mean everyone we see in the back street and the MALL.

We all have the right to everything we see, I mean we all do, you, all of them, and ME.

So when you see a bird, like a lonely and forgotten DOVE,
Remember, think about it, but do so with LOVE.

And when you sit down to EAT,
Remember there are people who don't even have a beet to EAT.

If your mother tongue is ENGLISH

Remember, there were many languages spoken when Columbus ARRIVED.

You may know, I say, you may know the name of one or two of them, but I'd be SURPRISED. So please give me the names of a couple of them that have SURVIVED.

Now, let's start thinking about things that have to CHANGE and I believe it's wide the RANGE.

To begin with, think about the NEWS. What do we see every day that gives us the BLUES?

I believe this is the right time and place, but only if we keep it up at a really good PACE.

So for now let's forget the president and let's just concentrate on Grace, that is Grace and RACE.

Et si ta langue maternelle est le Francais,

Souviens-toi que ce n'est pas la langue de tout le monde

Et que mic mac n'est pas un petit Big Mac.

C'est une langue qu'ont a PARLE au Quebec quand tes grands, grandparents sont ARRIVES.

And again, who were these people and why were they considered to be RED?

Thank goodness they're still around and their nation is not yet DEAD.

Y si eres de un pais AMERICANO puedes estar seguro que quando llegaste no eras un TEXANO,

Y si tu lengua materna es el ESPANOL, tampoco existia en tu pais "AT ALL."

NO, hace quinientos anos, tus papas lo TRAJERON, Sin saber que lo HICIERON.

Y si vienes de uno de los otros paisies quien sabe cuantos idiomas PERDIERON y que nunca

Mas VOLVIERON.

Y cuantos idiomas, hace miles de anos, se han PERDIDO y no los oyes ahora, ni LEIDOS.

But let's start and let's continue FOREVER, because if we don't start now, it may be NEVER!

And no matter where you're from, you may consider yourself black, white, yellow, or RED, but no matter what our color is, we are the same in our head, our bed, and when we're DEAD.

So let's begin to love everyone and forget about using a GUN. Don't you think that would be to our advantage, HUN?

Please think, don't groan, and always remember the planet. We can't live without it, damn it. But now we may be able to find or make another one, but in the meanwhile, We have to learn to take care of this one.

Portuguese, Romanesti, Italiano, Francais, Español, Arabic, English, and others—we all speak the tongue of our mothers. Stefan

THE SAINT AND CRYSTAL GRAND ROYAL PRINCESS, UM BANAT D'OOH (UB)

E ARLY IN THE century, two of the only three surviving royalty from the land of Ooh on the planet N'dikxix/9 in a faraway uncharted galaxy were sent into exile during an ethnic uprising, which was turning into a devastating interplanetary war. One princess stayed in Ooh, one was sent in the opposite direction from our galaxy, and one, the Saint and Crystal Grand Royal Princes, Um Banat d'Ooh (UB), was sent to a planet, somewhere past our Earth, to the palace of a distant uncle where she would be safe.

Unfortunately for her family, but fortunately for us, the intergalactic hibernation unit in which UB d'Ooh was traveling experienced technical difficulties just as the unit swirled between Mars and Earth on its path toward her uncle's planet, taking it very close to Earth. Just prior to entering the Earth's gravitational pull, the hibernation unit failed and UB came out of a deep, several light years' sleep. In her awakened state, she frenzied as she realized that she did not have enough oxygen* to make it to her uncle's kingdom. (*Surprisingly enough, the Oohan word for oxygen, "Ooh'k-C-Jun," has the same etymology as the word used on Earth.) Through telepathy and as her brain was impacted by radio waves from various galaxies (Many originating in the past and future from Earth, including some from our days, such as Al-Jazeera, BBC, and CNN), she realized that in spite of the fact that many of the planet's leaders had little respect, in reality no special love for "Ooh'k-C-jun," there was still enough of it on Earth to support life.

It was too late to reprogram her unit, so she decided to crash-land on our planet and prayed for survival. From this point on, she depended on celestial beings to guide her.

Now, even though we may not be aware of it, it is important that we know that there is a constant coming and going of angels bending near the Earth, all of whom at that time were aware of UB's strife and mental preparation to meet her maker or to carry out his will. And all of whom, impressed by her goodness and likeness to themselves, decided to pluck her from the unit. As she rapidly approached crash-landing in the Empty Quarter of the Arabian Desert, her unit suddenly veered toward the *Middle White Sea (*Mediterranean). With a deafening boom, it cracked open like an oyster shell. Its pearl, enveloped in angel dust, was carefully posed on Earth at the most immediate point from where the unit opened, a very green area on the outskirts of the desert equidistant between Damascus and Acca (Acres).

Though stunned momentarily and made invisible by the angel dust, she regained her composure, unseen under a village date palm. As she was invisible, the occasional drops of nectar from the ripening dates above would fall on her forehead and appear to be suspended in air! When a honeybee landed on her invisible forehead to imbibe in the sweet drops, she was slightly tickled by the bee's tiny paws and tried to brush it aside. The angry bee then dove into the skin of the invisible princess and stung her. The initial burning of the sting returned visibility to the Princess's soft glowing skin and revived her.

At that very moment, the bee lost her stinger, became a queen herself, and flew into the atmosphere, where she seeded the clouds lingering over the hot dry village. This caused a gentle cool mist to cover the area for three days, a completely hitherto then unknown phenomena for the villagers. The joy of the coolness and the recently arrived saintliness brought to the village a mood so festive that the princess was invited into each home and made to feel part of the village.

The princess could not explain her real dilemma to the kind villagers, but merely told them that she had been banished from her village, the name of which she had forgotten due to very traumatic circumstances, which she had also forgotten. She grew to love the area and eventually

STEFAN TOMA

married. She had no children directly, because it was forbidden by her royal court to have heirs born of her womb. Real daughters on Earth could only be spiritually seeded daughters, which would be considered as her vrais daughters, born spiritually, through ancient mixtures of scriptures long lost to all but the three, UB and her two distant sisters. The spiritual insemination, known only through the royal house of her parents and, naturally, to those from above, began to work.

Eventually, UB married. Her husband was from Acca, where the two lived until 1948. During that time, UB came to know the Awads of Acca and she became especially fond of a beautiful young lady named Siham, later to become the mother of Rose, Randa, Rima, and Najib and the grandmother of Amalia, Marya, Rami, and Fouad.

In 1972, a young man from a distant continent spent a scant twenty-four hours in Damascus, where Princes dÒoh, now simply known as Mary or Maryam, lived with her Accan husband. Unbeknownst to the young man and to UB, the guardian angel of his mother, Evelyn, was the same angel who took care of Siham and who had saved the princess.

On the morning of his arrival in Damascus, angel dust from his mother polarized by angel dust from Siham swirled in multihalos around UB. She was immediately drawn toward the young man, whom she first spied from the distance as he stood stunned by the perfume emanating from the spice shops in the souq near the Umayyad Mosque, where it is said that the Christ child will one day return to Earth. Even though UB had special gifts and was aware of most things around her, she did not know why she had been drawn to the young man. She followed him, and in order to understand more about him, she touched her left eyelid with the small finger of her left hand. When the young man bent down to pick up something he had dropped, with the same finger, she brushed the top of his left ear. For the first time since her arrival on Earth, she became invisible again and remained so for ninety minutes. During this time, she was whisked back and forth between her ancient land of Ooh, Acca, Beirut, Damascus, and Phoenix in the desert land of the young man, where spiritually she became mixed and nearly one with Siham and Evelyn. At the end of the ninety minutes, she again touched the young man as he was leaving a curio shop named Giovanni's, At eighty-nine minutes and fifty-nine seconds of her astral voyage and spiritual sprint, she touched his right ear and regained her physical body. Exhausted, UB struggled to return to her home in Damascus. Fighting drowsiness which was never before known to her, she fought sleep until she made her way home, where she entered her bedroom and collapsed on the bed. As her head hit the pillow, the vision of several young ladies began to dance in her mind, shining like bright stars within her cerebral galaxy. She knew immediately that these girls were to be her true daughters: Evelyn and three paternal ladies-in-waiting, Emma, Ina Lee, and Margaret; her stepdaughters, Anita, Deborah, plus Siham and four ladies-in-waiting, Lamia, Soumaya, Violette, and Lily; her daughters Rose, Randa, and Rima; and her stepdaughter, Elda, the last and the one chosen to seal the pact between UB and her daughters on Earth (the bride of her son, Najib).

Because of her special situation on Earth, the royal court ordered that, even though UB may never have the chance to hold each of her daughters in her arms, she would be with them forever spiritually and would warm their souls whenever they were in need of warming. Notwithstanding the beautiful relationship UB knew she would enjoy from now on with her daughters. She wanted to confer some material tokens of her attachment to them. In a tattered bag that she kept constantly at her side, UB had guarded some broken pieces of plain but royal jewelry from her faraway home. It was the only material that she had kept at her side, even as she was hurled from her unit. The pieces were sent to local artisan who recrafted them according to the telepathic orders given by UB. They were then entrusted to the young man (not so young anymore) to be given to UB's daughters to always remember her by.

Those who received the necklaces should wear them often when in the company of sisters, especially on their own birthdays and always on the seventeenth of August, the day the last of UB's children was reborn.

A few minutes ago, somewhere in a poor neighbourhood in Damascus, an old but very handsome Accan has just learned of his wife's definitive departure from her adopted home. Although his love for her was more perfect than any love found on Earth, he could not grieve for her, as her presence will always be felt by him and his unseen daughters. In UB, he knows that their royal daughters are safe on Earth and that forever more their families and all that touch them would be destined to a special place. They would be lovers and protectors of the Earth and carry with them a special mission. Their children, their children's children, and so on would always toil toward making the Earth the planet God meant it to be, our wonderful and still developing village, planet EARTH.

I also want to mention that I was inspired to write by the daughters of Um Banat (the mother of girls), Siham, Lamia, Soumaya, Violette, Lily, Rose, Randa, Rima, Elda, Marya, Evelyn, Emma, Ina Lee, Margaret, Anita, Deborah, and Amalia. All WWs (Wonderful Women).

Thank you, Stefan

Mom and Dad

Mom and Dad

Mom and Dad

Rami and Amalia

Rose, Stefan and Rami

Rose and Amalia

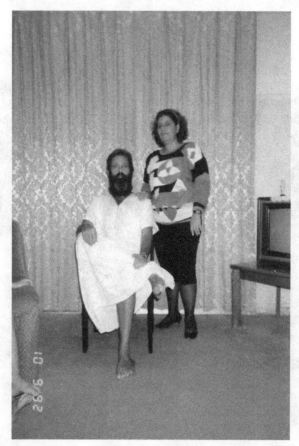

Rose and Stefan

Rose and Stefan

Rose

Danny and Rory
Rodrigo and Esteban

Where is Tchad?

Stefan hoping to fit in….

Stefan, Minkutu and family in Tchad

Oratory St Joseph in Montreal

CPSIA information can be obtained
at www.ICGtesting.com
Printed in the USA
LVHW031559050821
694493LV00004B/489